The Bitcoin Tao

The Bitcoin Tao

The Book of the Bitcoin Way and Its Virtue

Zach Wischler

Foreword by Robert Warren

Bitcoin Magazine Books
Nashville, TN

The Bitcoin Tao by Zach Wischler

ISBN 979-8-9999542-4-4 (Paperback)
ISBN 979-8-9999542-7-5 (eBook)
ISBN 979-8-9999542-5-1 (Limited Collector's Edition)

BITCOIN MAGAZINE BOOKS™

Published by Bitcoin Magazine Books
An imprint of BTC Inc.
6339 Charlotte Pike, Unit #B321, Nashville TN, 37209
Address all queries to contact@btcmedia.org

Interior design by MediaNeighbours.com
Illustrations by Lady Block Jane

To my father, who taught me low time preference long before I had a name for it.

Foreword

"All models are wrong, but some are useful." So goes the refrain from statistician George E.P. Box.

In Bitcoin, models overwhelm: moving averages (both exponential and simple), coin days destroyed, MVRV, SOPR, stock-to-flow, logarithmic regressions. To the early learner, it's a flood of emergent, magical lines on the price chart; a kind of techno-astrology that's *right enough* to mystify the eternally bullish.

Models, upon models, upon models self-reproduce in an ever-flowing stream of clicks and likes, and important discourse in the comments on the functional limits of the *Hot New Indicator (TM)* captivates the rabid data-lover.

Yet, models are not strictly confined to the numerical realm of the engineer or mathematician. There are also linguistic modelers and concept creators—the philosophers, the corporate executives, and even court jesters who paint on the cave walls of the collective Bitcoin consciousness. They trace the archetypal imagery of 750,000 lines of code. Archaic rubbings of peer-to-peer networks, a honey badger, encrypted walls of energy—even an etching of Venice?

Still, all these models are wrong, but some are useful. Right? Whether we speak the language of mathematics or metaphor, that base human urge is the same. We want to *relate* to Bitcoin. We want it to be personal, to be ours, to be understood in the way that we alone love and understand it.

And, like the Bitcoin obsessives we are, we want to burst forth and share that excitement with *you*.

Much to the bitcoiner's chagrin, our excitement, whether mathematical or metaphorical, comes off as a new, overeager parent. Simultaneously deep with the newfound wisdom of parenting, yet still immature enough to show you 30 photos of our baby while waiting in the Costco checkout line. Deep down, we *know* you don't really care. But we can't help ourselves. We love Bitcoin, so we model, we create, we celebrate, and we burst forth at the least opportune times.

This urge is not static. Just as the parent of the infant becomes the parent of the toddler, adolescent, and moody teenager, so too must early Bitcoin days evolve into what inevitably comes next.

The Bitcoin Tao is what comes next: a book beyond models. And this is why *The Bitcoin Tao* is a pleasure to read.

When Bitcoin has grown out of infancy into genuine self-reliance, and the naive excitement of the early models has been all but forgotten, we will finally find ourselves asking the important question of *what to do with the rest of our lives on the Bitcoin Standard.*

As the Mellencamp song goes, "Oh yeah, life goes on, long after the thrill of living is gone." Yet *The Bitcoin Tao* is not a childlike fit against growing up; it is not even a weathered cry to return to the "good old days" of Bitcoin. Instead, it is a quiet invitation for those ready to listen.

In the unpretentious, sacred language of the Tao, Wischler weaves deep technological understanding into a multi-thousand-year web of Taoist thought.

After every modern model and metaphor has been proven both wrong and useless, there remains only the question of understanding. And how better to understand than to merge the technical and philosophical? So the words of Lao-Tzu are brought to life anew. As Wischler puts it, "So the bitcoiner lives openly with cognitive dissonance and paradoxical understanding."

Maybe this is the greatest accomplishment of the work—how Wischler so confidently traverses early Bitcoin history, technical subtlety, the modern financial landscape, and ancient wisdom, while never once flinching in the face of paradox.

The Bitcoin Tao invokes no master archetype and presents no indicators. True to its textual inspiration, it states the paradox plainly, then gently asks you to sit with it. By refusing to make easy what is necessarily hard, or to make simple what is inherently complex, the book offers an opportunity and an invitation for actual understanding.

I recommend small doses: a bite in the morning, a few after dinner. The 81 sections are dense, rich. They melt in the mouth and are meant to be savored. Too many at once will undoubtedly leave your head spinning. Instead, treat this book like a box of fine chocolates. Have a taste, consider, share with a friend, discuss, then leave it on the counter for a moment lest you overwhelm the palate.

Come back to it when you can't resist any longer. Prolong the enjoyment.

And once you've finished, taste it again.

Robert Warren

Preface

There are many rules in Bitcoin.

This may seem obvious, given that it is a rules-based protocol. But there are also rules outside the protocol—spoken, yet unspoken—that bind those who find themselves drawn to it. Perhaps these aren't rules so much as shared principles. Cultural identities. The quiet understanding between strangers who have each, in their own way, fallen down the rabbit hole.

In reading the *Tao Te Ching*, I noticed the same paradox. On one hand, there are guidelines and themes that run true throughout its eighty-one verses. On the other hand, the very act of defining these principles is precisely what is advised against, making them so hard to grasp.

During the years I spent writing *The Bitcoin Tao*, I kept returning to this question: What are the general principles that make bitcoiners unique? What draws them together?

I found it remarkable that a protocol built on strict cryptographic rules must also, paradoxically, be willing to change. That a network designed for trustlessness creates such a profound community movement. That something so technical could inspire such philosophical depth.

It was in sitting with these contradictions that I gained some insights into my own life—namely, the ability to hold dear what I find true while remaining fiercely willing to change.

Throughout this book, I hope you will ponder not just Bitcoin, but what money is, what value is, and what we are trying to discover in this brief existence. The *Tao Te Ching* has guided seekers toward a more fulfilling life for millennia. It is my hope that through these verses of *The Bitcoin Tao*, you will see how Bitcoin can also become a guiding force for positive change in your life – and for billions of people yet to come.

Introduction

The idea for *The Bitcoin Tao* was simple. I was reading a verse of the *Tao Te Ching* one evening and noticed how philosophically similar it felt to Bitcoin. It was something about the paradoxes, the message of patience, and the way both reward those who can hold steadfast through difficulties without forcing resolution. I wrote a sample verse on a whim based on these ideas and was hooked.

If you are deep in Bitcoin culture, you will find inside jokes throughout: references to Laszlo's pizza, the $5 wrench attack, Patoshi patterns, the S9 in your garage, miners scaling up unsustainably, BTCSessions videos, the particular pain of watching BitMex liquidate your over-leveraged position. These are not explained in the text, so if you do not recognize a reference, I invite you to look it up in the Glossary. Consider it an invitation to explore the history and culture of Bitcoin's early days!

If you are new to Bitcoin, the book will still hopefully make sense. The deeper teachings that matter are about patience, discipline, humility, and the difference between knowledge and wisdom. These do not require technical fluency to appreciate, and you will likely absorb more with each re-read as your understanding grows. The *Tao Te Ching* works in a similar way.

A note on the various lessons mentioned throughout the book. Many of these verses are warnings I wish I had received sooner. Most of what I share here, I learned the hard way: trading emotionally or with leverage, chasing altcoin returns or yield, trusting custodians, and speaking too confidently or too early about a viewpoint. I have made these mistakes, or watched people close to me make them. Pain is a great teacher. It is the other side of the same coin as reward.

"Tao" simply means "the way." This is a text about the way of Bitcoin: its principles, practices, and paradoxes. It is also, I hope, a book about the way of living well. With patience. With discipline. With low time preference. And with enough humility to know that the market and, to a greater degree, life, will find a way to teach you what you may refuse to learn on your own.

This book contains 81 verses, and there is no correct order in which to read them. Read it however you like. Keep it on your desk. Flip to a verse when you need a reminder. You may find, as I have, that the lessons bear revisiting—I've been surprised at just how many I've had to relearn since discovering Bitcoin.

Thank you for taking the time to read *The Bitcoin Tao.* I hope you find within it insight, humor, and something worth returning to.

P.S. The verses were written chronologically over two years, between 2023 and 2025. Because of this, you might notice themes that recur based on what was happening in Bitcoin at the time. The earlier verses were written when Ordinals first emerged. The latter verses came amid concerns about quantum computing, scaling debates, the Bitcoin Core controversy, ETFs and treasury companies, and a general sense that Bitcoin's path forward felt less certain than before. And yet, paradoxically, it still feels certain. Bitcoin has always been uncertain, but my own mindset shifted as I wrote it too, drifting toward something closer to Taoist acceptance: of cycles, of patience, of trust in the process even when the road ahead is unclear.

ONE

The coin that can be forked
is not the eternal coin.
The chain that can be 51% attacked
is not the eternal chain.

The coin is both real and imagined.
As real, it is the root of 10,000 Merkle trees;
as imagined, it is the coinbase of the genesis block.

Ever ticking, one can see the timechain;
Ever stacking, one sees only low time preference.
And the peer-to-peer connection is the tunnel to all
consensus.

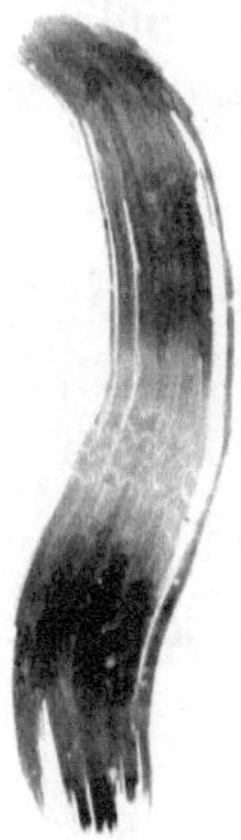

TWO

In Bitcoin, all can see consensus as true,
only because there are hard forks.
All know compatible upgrades are good,
only because there are chain-splits.

Spending and receiving bitcoin just
reorganizes the UTXO set.
The difficulty adjusts when mining is easy.
Long confirmation times are defined by short,
high fee rates by the sub-sat/vB era.
Before and after Segwit upgrades
are compatible with each other.

So the bitcoiner lives openly with cognitive dissonance
and paradoxical understanding.
They can sign transactions offline
and HODL without effort.
Holding onto UTXOs without losing them,
he works, but not for block rewards;
he mines, but not for economic profits.

When the header is found,
the work is indexed to the longest chain.
That is why it lasts forever.

THREE

Putting fiat value on satoshis
will create weak hands.
If you promote altcoins, people will get rugged.
By not displaying how much you're stacking,
you will keep $5 wrench attacks at bay.

The bitcoiner acts
by clearing the mempool and consolidating UTXOs,
by weakening FUD narratives
and strengthening hashrate.

Practice not trading…
When action is patient and aligned with incentives,
every satoshi ends up in the right wallet address.

FOUR

The mempool is empty but inexhaustible,
bottomless,
the beginning of it all.

Within it, pending outputs can be spent;
confirmation times ebb and flow;
difficulty is predicted through the adjustment period;
transactions settle into place.

It is shared but individual.
I do not know who gave it a default 300 MB limit.
It seems to be the common ancestor of all,
the father of confirmed blocks.

FIVE

The miners and plebs are impartial;
They see the first 10,000 inscriptions
as part of the UTXO set.
The bitcoiner is not sentimental;
he treats all his coins as fungible.

The ordinal number is like
the block confirmation height:
no number is especially dear,
nor is any one disfavored.
He spends and replaces, without condition,
offering sound money to everyone.

Inside taproot transactions and witness data is spam;
unprunable and unstoppable,
the more it is used, the longer IBD takes.

Hold on to the seed phrase.
Man was made to sit in amazement at the difficulty
of solving the discrete log problem.

SIX

The bitcoiner that lives forever
is called the spirit of Satoshi.
Although they have no control over the protocol,
their initial gift is never lost.
Although many have declared themselves as him,
their true pseudonymity remains.

The evidence of the mysterious Satoshi
is within the scriptSig of the genesis block.

Listen to the coinbase of each block,
hear its echo through gossip of the nodes.
Without fail, it reveals the decreasing subsidy.
Without fail, the halvings
bring us into low time preference.
Although the cycles are predictable,
they recur; fear and greed will never end.

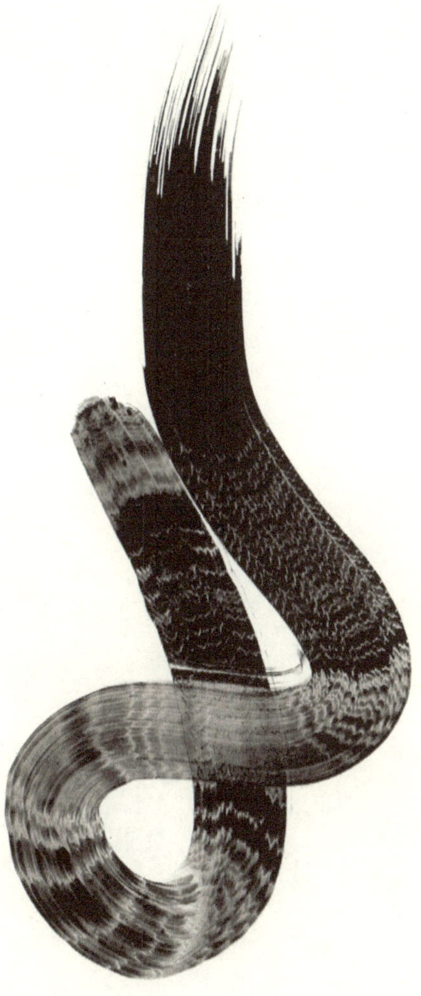

SEVEN

Bitcoin is eternal—the blockchain endures.
Why will Bitcoin and its blockchain last forever?
It does not exist for Cantillionaires only.
That is the secret of its durability.

For this reason, the bitcoiner spends his sats last,
and receives the highest value.
His transaction data stays segregated from the witness,
so he pays less in fees.

Serve the needs of the network,
and incentives will take care of the rest.
Through guerrilla mining,
no-KYC bitcoin is attained.

EIGHT

The supreme bitcoiner is like a B-cash maxi,
who circulates all UTXOs without trying to.
Their coins are used as a medium of exchange
where possible.
Therefore, they are like Laszlo.

Use bitcoin in accordance with peer-to-peer cash.
In spending, be aware of coin days destroyed.
In UTXO consolidation, first go deep in Chainalysis.
In receiving from others,
provide both QR and copy/paste options.
Stand by never re-using addresses.
Govern updates with your own node.
Be timely in broadcasting transactions.

One who operates in accordance
with the longest chain of work
does not go against the way of consensus.
He moves in harmony with the current fee rate,
always knowing the right sat/vB amount to pay.

NINE

To keep on borrowing
is not as good as HODLing.
Over-leveraged, BitMex will margin call you,
better to stop trading with 100x.

Use an address too much
and its anonymity will be lost.
Fill your wallet with rare runes and inscriptions
and it brings about high time preference.
Brag about altcoin returns to X followers
and no one can save you from a rug-pull.

Wait until six block confirmations have passed;
this is the way of the bitcoiner.

TEN

Carrying ColdCard and node
and embracing the current fee rate,
can you avoid flagging RBF?

Can you leave your UTXOs
as untouched as a newbie's on Coinbase?
In the opening and closing of lightning channels,
can you play the cooperative partner?

Can you empower your Bitcoin community
and run a local meetup group
without self-importance?

Spending sats and DCA'ing;
cold-storage, yet not losing it;
evangelizing, yet not inspiring greed;
submitting a pull request as a nym.

One who heeds this advice
brings the Bitcoin economy to life.
This is the world under sound money.

ELEVEN

Thirty lightning channels
converge upon a single routing hub;
it is on the node in the center that
the useful liquidity hinges.

Construct inputs into a PSBT;
it is the space in the signature that makes it useful.
Mint inscriptions and Counterparty NFTs,
but the UTXO is useful in its fungibility.

The usefulness of what is consensus
depends on what is breaking.

TWELVE

The five keys lock the multisig script.
The five nodes open the ring channel.
The five ASICs heat the home.
The airdrops and altcoins awaken people's greed.

Wasting whole coins to obtain rare NFTs
only slows one's DCA.

The bitcoiner observes the miner's signaling period
but trusts his own full node.
He allows "Bitcoin 2.0" narratives to come and go.
He prefers what is within his control to what is outside.

THIRTEEN

Influencers and groupthink are alarming.
A high follower count greatly distorts your perception.

Why are influencers and groupthink alarming?
Seeking followers is a confirmation bias:
alarming when they are gained,
alarming when they are lost.

Why does a high number of followers
greatly cloud your rationality?
The reason we have a lot of echo chambers
is that we have social media algorithms.
If we had no influencers,
what pump and dumps would we have?

Man's best tweets are eternal,
yet he thinks, I am this nym and will soon be forgotten.
If we have no internet archive,
what receipts would we have?
One who sees himself as an individual
is fit to run a sovereign node.
One who spreads knowledge with humility
is fit to be a YouTube educator like BTCSessions.

FOURTEEN

That which has not been authorized is called unsigned.
That which cannot be heard has not been broadcasted.
That which cannot be honored is called unconfirmed.
These three cannot be trusted;
therefore, they are evidenced as false.

Each of these three
is subtle in description.
By intuition you can
sign it, broadcast it, and confirm it.
Then the unsigned, offline, and unconfirmed
are presented as one.

Its gossip brings no new blocks,
its confirmation no double-spend;
It goes on and on,
unnameable,
returning to the UTXO set.

Do not sign and there is no transaction,
use KYC and there is no end to its trail.
You cannot know it, but you can HODL it,
under protection of your own private key.

Discovering the history of the protocol development
brings one into understanding of governance today.

FIFTEEN

The OG bitcoiners were profound and visionary.
Their wisdom was unthinkable.
There is no way to describe their risk tolerance.
One can only describe them vaguely by their nym.

Watchful, like noderunners during a soft-fork period.
Alert, like devs peer reviewing BIPs.
Simple as Turing incompleteness.
Hollow like the conviction of altcoiners.
Yielding, like the custodians who collapse
each halving cycle.
Amorphous, like a jointly-held shared delusion
we all have.

But the most disjointed of ideas reveals strength
as it is gossiped.
And out of the gossip,
consensus arises.

He who spends bitcoin does not want blocks to be full.
But precisely because they are never full,
he can mine patiently off-grid,
and does not rush for frantic hashrate accumulation.

SIXTEEN

Become totally empty.
Let the mempool clear.
Amidst the rush of daily transactions,
observe how inputs become outputs.

Blocks confirm, each by each,
only to index to the chaintip . . .
to what is settled, and what has yet to be.

To confirm your own deposits is to run an economic node.
To run economic nodes is to accept or reject changes.
To accept or reject changes is to uphold consensus.
To uphold consensus is the work of a true bitcoiner.
Not knowing this cycle
leads to eternal hard forks.

Knowing the protocol rules gives consensus.
This consensus is distributed.
Distributed consensus is the highest security;
the highest security is Bitcoin.

Using bitcoin, your transactions will be in sync
with your peers.
Being in sync with your peers is essential.
This ledger is everlasting,
not endangered by the death of fiat currencies.

SEVENTEEN

With the greatest monetary asset before them,
people barely know one exists.
Next comes one with high-yield rates.
Next comes one with untenable inflation.
Next comes one with complete capital controls.

When a central bank controls the money,
no one trusts it.

The wise bitcoiner worries little.
He never spends carelessly.
He mines for network security
and leaves no CO_2 emissions.
When the hash is confirmed, the people say,
"Tick tock, next block."

EIGHTEEN

When the hardness of Bitcoin is present,
value arises from one's proof of work.
When the hardness of Bitcoin is absent,
value comes from subjective definitions
of stable prices and maximum employment.

If you need stable prices and maximum employment
for functioning money,
if you act with moral hazard,
this is a sure sign that hard money is absent.
Thus we see the great monetary trilemma.

When currency falls into fractionalization,
inflation and entitlement programs arise.
When the country falls into hyperinflation,
totalitarian leaders will appear;
revolution is born.

NINETEEN

Give up trading, renounce shitcoinery,
and it will be a hundred times better for everyone.
Throw away forks and airdrops
and people will do the right thing.
Forget about ICOs and tokenomics
and there will be no scams.

All of these are fiat money behaviors,
they are not noble in intent.

It is more important to see the opportunity,
to realize Bitcoin's true purpose for humanity,
to cast off high time preference and temper greedy desire.

TWENTY

Give up the fiat lifestyle and you will be free
from all your struggles.
What is the difference between Bitcoin and fiat?
What is the difference between good money and bad?

Must I fear what others fear?
Should I fear bank runs
when there is verifiable self-custody?
Should I fear fractionalization,
when my node is confirming the UTXO set?

In "DeFi summer," some go to casinos to trade altcoins,
but I am alone stacking sats, not knowing
how close I am to my long-term HODL goal.
Like a nocoiner before they learn to run a node,
I am alone, without a mempool of my own
to broadcast from.

Most people have too many coins;
I alone seem to be missing diversification.
My holdings are that of a "bell-curver"
in its highly concentrated allocation.
I am but a pleb in this world.
While others rush to trade with leverage,
I accept my humble DCA.

I alone seem foolish,
stacking sats, spending less.

Other people strive for Twitter fame,
I avoid the Recommended tab,
preferring to be left anon.
Indeed, I seem like an idiot:
no altcoins, no worries.

I can change like an unconfirmed transaction.
I move intuitively like hashrate during wet season.

All UTXOs settle after six confirmations.
Yet I can be stubborn and trust at Zero-conf.
But wherein I am most different from influencers is
in knowing to only stack the orange coin into self-custody!

TWENTY-ONE

The greatest savings strategy is to stack sats and sats alone.

Satoshis are indivisible and intangible.
Although indivisible and intangible,
it gives rise to hard money.
Although distributed and opt-in,
it gives rise to consensus.
Although technical and obscure,
it is the money, the store of value,
the medium of all exchanges.

Throughout the halvings, its code has been preserved
in order to follow the genesis block.
How do I know the ways of consensus at the beginning?
I look inside my full node and see what rules are within it.

TWENTY-TWO

The miners are balanced through halvings.
The unprofitable shut down.
The empty mempool is filled.
The S9's life is renewed.
The plebs are tested.
The whales are speculating.

Therefore the bitcoiner embraces increased difficulty.
Because he doesn't unplug miners,
people can hear his hashing.
Because he doesn't mine for reputation,
people can trust his intentions.
Because he doesn't call himself a "Bitcoin maxi"
altcoiners recognize themselves in him.
Because he has no fiat profit in mind,
everything he does succeeds.

The old saying that the plebs are the hodlers
of last resort is surely right!
If you have continually found block rewards
hashrate will flock to your pool.

TWENTY-THREE

To talk little about Bitcoin is natural:
Miners do not overclock in summertime bear markets;
a China ban does not last forever.
What does this? Incentives.

But these are exaggerated, forced effects,
and that is why they cannot be sustained.
If the largest hashrate pools cannot sustain a lucky streak,
how much less is a solo miner able to do?

Those who follow the incentives,
benefit from the incentives.

Those who follow humility
become humble themselves.
Those who stray from incentives and decency
become one with failure and scams.

If you go along with incentives,
harmony flows through you.
Your actions become self-sustaining,
your ways those of a flywheel.

Open your mind to Bitcoin
and trust your instinct about the perils of fiat currency...
then everything will start to fall into place.

TWENTY-FOUR

If you trade with leverage, you cannot HODL forever.
If you hold too many UTXOs, you cannot transact cheaply.

Accumulating extra hashrate does not reveal strength.
Promoting scams will not produce sustained wealth.
He who has high time preference is not disciplined.
He who shortcuts will not endure.

All these ways of acting are shitcoinery, distasteful.
They are unnecessary excesses.
They are like a split in the chain,
a fork in consensus.

When walking the path of the bitcoiner,
this is the very behavior that must be overcome,
discarded, and left behind.

TWENTY-FIVE

There was something hard and stable
after fiat money was born.
It is virtuous. Invisible.
Unique. Unchanging.
Always-on. Eternally ticking.
It is the Mother of sound money.
For lack of a better name,
I call it Bitcoin.

I call it sound money.
Sound money is borderless;
borderless is ever circulating;
ever circulating, it is constantly cycling new UTXOs.

Therefore, Bitcoin is great,
sound money is great,
circular economy is great.
bitcoiners are great.

Thus to know bitcoiners,
understand incentives.
To know incentives,
understand *Human Action.*
To know *Human Action*,
understand first principles.

TWENTY-SIX

The unspent is the root of the mempool.
The unconfirmed is the master of RBF.

Realizing this,
the savvy bitcoiner is
patient and not greedy
in the midst of all transactions;
although surrounded by high fees,
he is not swayed.

Why should the OG
move funds during business hours?
If you've been hodling for decades,
another few blocks is trivial.
To lose patience is to overpay for one's transactions.

TWENTY-SEVEN

A knower of Chainalysis
spends without combining inputs,
broadcasts without change outputs,
donates to FOSS projects without keeping an account.
The coins he holds, having no history,
cannot be traced.
The exchange he uses, though having low limits,
does not require KYC.

Be genuine and help all newcomers impartially,
recommending KYC to none.
Waste no fees on trading.
This is called DCA'ing every day.

What is an OG but an early UTXO hodler?
What is a fiat man but those without
a stack in their possession?
If the OG's wisdom is not respected,
and the beginner not appropriately warned,
they can "get into crypto," no matter how smart one is.
This is the great secret of the Bitcoin Tao.

TWENTY-EIGHT

Know the strength of six confirmations,
but keep a pending transaction's care.
Mine solo or in a pool;
if you do, your sovereign hashrate
will not fade away.
One can become like Patoshi again.

Know the block subsidy,
keep to the transaction fees,
and be a guerrilla miner of the world.
To be the guerrilla miner of the world is
to mine 24/7 during dry or wet season,
without ever unplugging,
and to return again to find the hash of the next block.

One who understands pool payout methods
while holding onto profit
acts in accordance with long-term sustainability.
To be the miner of all transactions
is to live the abundant life of an OFAC-denier.

When the plebs mine with BitAxes,
its profitability is irrelevant.
If you run your own hashrate,
you can confirm any transaction.

Truly, the solo miner spends least.

TWENTY-NINE

Do you think you can 51% attack the blockchain
and destroy it?
I do not believe it can be done.

Every miner plugged in is a sovereign vote
and cannot be controlled.
Trying to hard fork leads to ruin.
Rushing through Speedy Trial, we lose.

Allow network upgrades to merge naturally.
Know that it too is a function of incentives.
Just as the miners buy brand new ASICs, and then unplug,
there is a time for overclocking
and a time for shutting down;
a time for accumulating hashrate
and a time for selling the rip;
a time for expanding your operation
and a time for downsizing its scale;
a time for DCA'ing
and a time for saying YOLO.

To the bitcoiner
every block is a movement toward freedom,
so what need has he,
for the pump and dumps, leverage, or cycle extremes?

THIRTY

One who would guide a newcomer to sovereignty
will warn him against the use of altcoins for "innovation."
Reputation often turns upon the grifters.

Where "Bitcoin 2.0s" are bred,
blockchains offer nothing but rugpulls and vulnerabilities.
After a great hack has occurred,
the industry is cursed, the developer mindshare decreases,
the blockchain lies stripped of its security.

After you have hit your HODL number,
you must not talk about your bitcoin,
you must not boast of "how early you got in,"
you must not act like an "OG";
you must rather regret that you had not been
able to hasten adoption.

You must never think of accumulating bitcoin
by dishonesty.
Whatever is acquired with deception
will soon wither away.
It is not attuned to the low time preference.
Not being attuned to long-term incentives,
its end comes all too soon.

THIRTY-ONE

Griefing attacks are the tools of bad actors;
all honest noderunners detest them.
Therefore, bitcoiners never open channels with them.

Chainalysis serves evil.
They are a tool of those who oppose privacy.
Use their services only as a last resort.
For sovereignty and freedom are dearest
to the real bitcoiner's heart,
and to them even a Bitcoin Strategic Reserve
is no cause for rejoicing.

He who thinks airdrops are free money
is one with a will to kill Bitcoin
and one with a will to kill Bitcoin
shall never prevail upon the peer-to-peer economy.

It is a good sign when a high fee comes forward.
A bad sign when the mempool clears.

With the survival of hard forks and altcoins,
we have grifters and scammers.
Every airdrop is a lost cause;
when you win free money,
you celebrate by donating to OpenSats.

THIRTY-TWO

The Bitcoin Protocol has no ruler.
Although open and transparent,
no one in the world can control it.

If mining pools and developers could dictate it,
the 10,000 transactions in the mempool
would naturally end.
Bankers and Cantillionaires would rejoice
with the sounds of freshly printed fiat.
Everyone would live in serfdom,
not by their choice,
but by governmental decree.

Once the money is fractionalized, the coin needs yield.
There is already enough yield;
know when to stop printing.
Know when yield has limits
to prevent dilution of intrinsic value.

Central banks and government are born of weak money,
and all monetary hardness is born of shared rules.
Just as all weak money eventually fails from depreciation,
all bitcoin grows because of a finitely scarce amount.

THIRTY-THREE

One who reads the whitepaper has knowledge;
one who accepts bitcoin for payments has wisdom.
Block reorganization requires force;
surviving a bear market needs strength.

If you realize that you have enough bitcoin,
you are already rich.

One who pays in bitcoin surely lives long.
One who endows bitcoin for future generations,
surely lives on forever.

THIRTY-FOUR

The Bitcoin Protocol is universal;
it can apply to the pleb or the whale.
All users depend on it for settlement;
even so, it does not take credit for 99.9899% uptime.

It accomplishes its purpose,
but has no marketing team for itself.
It confirms all transactions abiding by the rules,
but does not ask what purpose they are for.

All blocks refer to it as their home,
but it does not have a favorite one;
thus it may be called "blockchain."

The bitcoiner imitates this conduct:
By not repeating scams of "blockchain technology"
the bitcoiner proclaims sound money.

THIRTY-FIVE

All virtues will come to those
who hold the orange coin.
They flock to it and receive no debasement,
for in it they find a transparent, unchanging
monetary system.

Altcoins and NFTs are fun and games,
yet they cause people harm.
How distracting and counterproductive
are cryptocurrency projects
when one compares them to Bitcoin!

When you look for it, there is nothing to see
but the longest chain of work.
When you listen for it, there is nothing to hear
but the confirmation sounds on mempool.space.
When you use it, the outputs reorganize themselves
back into the UTXO set.

THIRTY-SIX

Should you want to stop scams,
you must deliberately let them fail.
Should you want to weaken the altcoin narrative,
you must deliberately let them accept VC money.
Should you want to steer others toward Bitcoin-only,
you must deliberately let them come to it on their own.
Should you want to encourage decentralization,
you must deliberately grant others access to audit the code.

The lesson here is called
the wisdom of the bitcoiner.
The fair distribution model outlasts the greed.
The patient outlasts the hurried.

Nodes cannot confirm another chain,
and a wallet's extended public key
should never be displayed.

THIRTY-SEVEN

The UTXO is whole
and cannot be partially spent.
If humanity would
use them as a medium of exchange,
the global economy would be transformed
by itself, through natural incentives.

When transactions are transparent
and trust is not required,
maximum productivity shines through.

By not needing an inflationary currency,
the entire wealth gap problem will straighten itself out.
When there is sound money,
an economy anchors to maximum long-term
productivity growth rate.

THIRTY-EIGHT

A truly sovereign man holds his own private keys
and is therefore in control of his money.
A foolish man uses custodial wallets
and is therefore not sovereign.

The master HODLer doesn't trade,
and he accumulates wealth through DCAing.
The newbie is always buying and selling,
yet does not meaningfully increase his long-term position.

The highest virtue is to HODL without bragging.
The highest kindness is to donate
to open-source development anonymously.
The highest justice is to let others learn
from their own mistakes.

When sovereignty is lost, there is asking for permission.
When asking for permission is lost,
there are prohibited actions.
When prohibited actions are created, there is unrest.
Unrest is the husk of true freedom,
the beginning of a change in regime.

The Sovereign Individual follows his own nature
and not the laws or rules of government.

It is said:
"He runs his own node and doesn't use others."
"He signs PSBTs offline and won't touch hot wallets."
"He talks about Bitcoin but not his bitcoin."

THIRTY-NINE

These things are true since the genesis block:
The code is whole and complete.
The comments are whole and detailed.
The review process is whole and thorough.
The 10,000 mailing list developers are whole,
and the country is stacking a Strategic Bitcoin Reserve.
All these are because of Wholecoiners.

When man interferes with Bitcoin's code too much,
the chain starts splitting,
the nodes gossip weakens,
the security assumptions crumble,
and peer-to-peer money becomes extinct.

Therefore, the developer is rooted in caution;
good code accounts for human error.
This is why humble bitcoiners refer to themselves
as plebs, nyms, and anons.

The code of a developer is useless
unless it works in accordance with consensus.
A developer's updates bring no progress
unless it is accepted by the majority of their peers.

Playing one's role
in hyperbitcoinization
is true humility.

Truly, too much reputation means no reputation.
It is not wise to shine like gold
and resound like the stone Moai.

FORTY

Returning is the way of the UTXO.
Yielding is the way of the mempool.
The entire UTXO set is born of the coinbase.
Durability is rooted in intangibility.

FORTY-ONE

A great scholar hears of Bitcoin
and begins diligent UTXO management in self-custody.
A middling scholar hears of Bitcoin
and buys the ETF to get exposure.
An inferior scholar hears of Bitcoin
and calls it a scam.
Without that doubt, it wouldn't be Bitcoin.

So there are constructive sayings on this:
You buy bitcoin at the price you deserve,
going all in is opting out,
getting on zero fiat is the goal,
true saving seems like speculation,
cryptocurrency is clouded with scams,
transparent monetary policy seems "too technical,"
the greatest tool seems simple,
the greatest HODLers are indifferent to price,
the wisdom of DCA seems foolish.

Bitcoin's success is slow and inevitable
its code alone brings in a new era of monetary freedom.

FORTY-TWO

David Chaum created eCash.
From eCash came B-money and Hashcash.
After Hashcash came Bitcoin.
All three predated the 10,000 coins on CoinMarketCap.
The altcoins have pre-mines and
venture capital allocations;
they use you as exit liquidity by combining these forces.

People suffer at the thought of being
without diversification, without insurance,
or without composability.
Yet this is exactly the way that
Satoshi once described the protocol.
For one gains assurance by losing complexity,
And loses bitcoin by putting money into alts.

What OG HODLers taught, I teach.
The good money drives out the bad: Thiers' Law.
This is my fundamental teaching.

FORTY-THREE

The most intangible of all money
overrides the hardest of all metals.
That without substance preserves
where there is no space for destruction.
Hence I know the value of a digital storage of value.

Spreading adoption without words,
DCAing without action in my trading account—
few in the world can grasp its simplicity—
that is the HODLer's way.
Rare are those indeed
who can accumulate 6.15 Bitcoin without selling.

FORTY-FOUR

What means more to you,
your current losses or future gains?
What adds more to your net worth,
trading acumen or a buy-and-hold strategy?
I say what you gain in complexity,
is what you lose in effectiveness.

Wealth is the fruit of savings and discipline.
HODLing bitcoin is the result of
unwavering conviction and 10,000 hours of studying.

A confident bitcoiner doesn't panic during crashes.
He who knows when to buy the dip
is preserved from panic selling,
only then can you endure to see
gains from future halvings.

FORTY-FIVE

The perfect money seems imperfect,
and yet its use cases are limitless.
It does not have a venture backing,
and yet its upside is parabolic.

Great monetary policy seems confusing.
Great inventions seem like fads.
Great investments seem risky.
Great truths seem false.
Great revolution seems disorganized.

Supply cap conquers inflation;
Transaction fees surpass block subsidies.
Using bitcoin as a medium of exchange
and unit of account
is the next step for civilization.

FORTY-SIX

When the people have bitcoin,
they can save and plan for the future.
When the people lack bitcoin,
their savings and standards of living erode.

There is no greater loss
than trading time for infinite money,
no greater crime than inflation,
no greater tragedy than ignorance of fiat money;
the worst of tricks is working more yet
getting less over time.

Bitcoin savings alone is enough.
Indeed, the freedom from government tyranny
can be found in your own private keys.

FORTY-SEVEN

Without broadcasting a transaction,
know its uncensorability.
Without having read *The 7th Property*,
you may know the path to financial freedom.

The farther down the rabbit hole one goes,
the less one knows.
Therefore the bitcoiner does not study
and yet understands sound money intuitively.
He does not strive to outperform DCA
and yet his stacking goal is still attained.

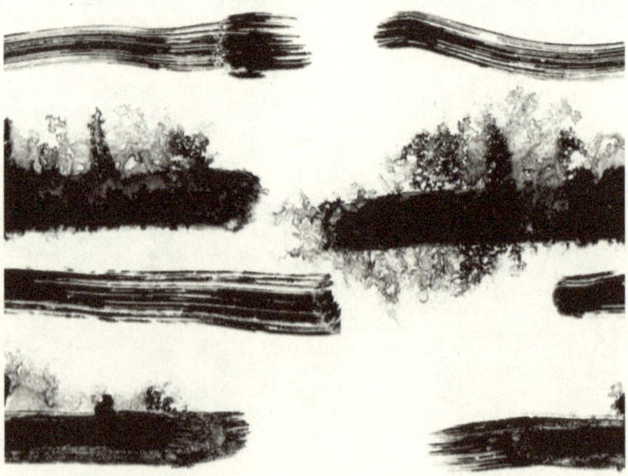

FORTY-EIGHT

Stacking sats consists of daily accumulating.
Getting on zero fiat consists of daily diminishing;
selling fiat to unplug from the matrix,
until no paper money remains.
When zero fiat is reached,
no personal value is left to be inflated away.

True Bitcoin adoption can be reached
by letting the pain of inflation become unignorable.
It cannot be achieved by force or interference.

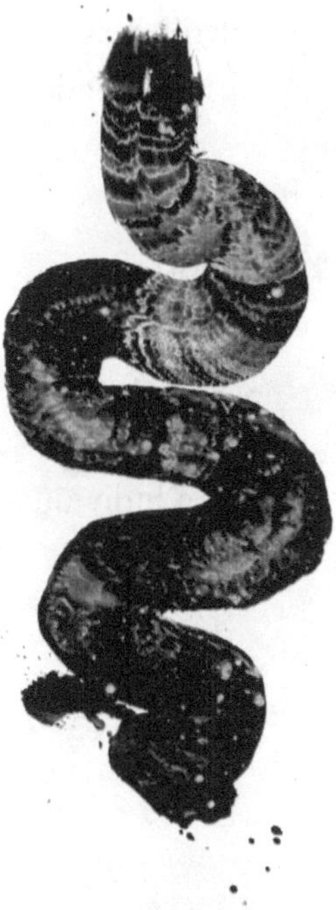

FORTY-NINE

The bitcoiner has no fixed price target;
he is aware of the laws of supply and demand.

Those who promote Bitcoin he treats with reverence.
Those who attack Bitcoin he also treats with reverence
because Bitcoin's path to monetization is assured.

He is kind to the plebs.
He is also kind to the shitcoiners,
because the nature of a bitcoiner
is community.

He is loyal to his local Bitcoin meetup,
but is also loyal to his normie friends.
He lives in harmony
through the Fourth Turning.
He sees everything as a season;
each saeculum, a role to play.

All freedoms will be afforded to him.
He behaves like a Sovereign Individual.

FIFTY

Between bitcoiners today,
three in ten are users of custodians;
three in ten hold equity in treasury companies.
And those who "just buy the ETF instead"
also number three in ten.

Why is this so?
Because they clutch to the familiar
and cling to their old, antiquated ways.

But there is one in ten, they say, so sure of self-custody
that class action lawsuits and capital gains
will never afflict him.
Dusters add more sats to his wallet,
he got off Gox before it collapsed,
he never lent his coins to BlockFi,
and rumor has it, he does not care about yield.

Why is this so?
Because self-custody makes your wealth invincible,
when life's opportunities can not be robbed
through moral hazard or inflation.

Realize the once-in-a-species discovery
and your legacy will last for generations.

FIFTY-ONE

Bitcoin connects all humans
under one fair monetary system.
It sprung into existence in 2009,
pseudonymously, near perfect, to promote freedom;
It took on a life of its own;
let exponentially-growing hashrate secure its future.

Therefore all beings can recognize its independence
and value its savings power.
They have not been forced to hold bitcoin,
but do so by choice, out of rational economic incentives.

Bitcoin gives them hope.
Its purchasing power preservation
nourishes and protects their livelihoods.
Bitcoin creates opportunities and not oppression;
equivocally open to all;
unites others through simple protocol rules;
and aligns citizen incentives across the world.
This is called the peaceful revolution.

FIFTY-TWO

All those holding bitcoin have a common beginning.
This beginning is
understanding the Federal Reserve System.
Having known the "hamster wheel" arrangement
we're put on,
we may proceed to look for alternatives.
Having known a taste of freedom,
we should convert all our fiat to hard money.

Don't talk about your bitcoin,
guard your private keys
and wealth will be accumulated.
Talk about your stack,
brag with lambos and high time preference behavior,
and your bitcoin won't be yours for long.

Seeing value in the smallest unit
account is called "Sats the Standard."
HODLing through multiple halvings in self-custody
is called having "diamond hands."
Following the verifiable truth
will save you from misfortune.

This is called
don't trust, verify.

FIFTY-THREE

If I have even just a little sense,
I should buy some bitcoin just in case it catches on,
and my only fear would be being too late.

Accumulating bitcoin is simple and easy,
yet the people prefer devious paths.
That is why the Federal Reserve is corrupt,
Congressmembers engage in insider trading,
and the debt ceiling is infinite.

Flying private jets,
wearing fancy jewelry,
indulging in the finest food and drink,
amassing a large bitcoin fortune
to the extent of not knowing what to do with it,
is being like a Cantillionaire.

I say this lifestyle at the expense of others
is like bragging on X after a rugpull.
This is not the Bitcoin Tao.

FIFTY-FOUR

Whoever's savings are in bitcoin
will not be inflated away.
Whoever embraces DCA & self-custody
will not be left behind.

Generations will revere your hodl strategy.
Rooted in low time preference, opportunity is realized;
based on not trusting but verifying,
conviction strengthens;
cultivated in a local community, momentum increases;
rooted in a desire to separate money from state,
freedom for all abounds.

Bitcoin is everywhere;
it will become synonymous with "money."
To truly understand it, see it is a breakthrough.
In a person, see it as a tool for sovereignty;
in a family, see it as a means of support;
in a country, see it as a vessel for opportunity;
in the world, see it as a movement toward freedom.

How do I know this is true?
I've spent thousands of hours studying Bitcoin.

FIFTY-FIVE

He whose node is in consensus with their peers
is like a sovereign citizen.
Corrupt governments will not stop his transactions.
Miners will not reject his pool shares.
Block reorganizations will not affect him.
His data usage is minimal, his hard drive space aplenty,
yet his freedom to transact is unmatched.

He may not have ever flagged RBF or CPFP,
but knows his ordering of transactions is correct.
His reliability is high.
He runs his node 24/7 without overheating.
He doesn't use a Raspberry Pi.

To know the block height is to know
the most recent timestamp;
to know the current hashprice
is to have insight into mining conditions.
Things in harmony with reinforcing incentives remain;
things that are forced may last for a while,
but then fade away.
This is not the Bitcoin Tao.
And whatever is against the Bitcoin Tao soon becomes
another data point of "Bitcoiners were right again."

FIFTY-SIX

Those who stack sats do not worry.
Those who worry do not stack sats.

Sell all of your fiat!
Close your bank account,
spend the cash beneath your mattress,
empty your vault of gold,
strengthen your conviction,
teach the importance of self-custody,
sell your chairs.
This is going all in on a once-in-a-species invention.

One who realizes this opportunity
is not scared off by narratives or volatility,
swayed by unrealized profit or loss,
nor caught up in the scams on CoinMarketCap.
He is far beyond your 100x day trader
yet has a bigger stack than they ever will.

Thus, being a bitcoin-only HODLer
is the highest-returning savings strategy.

FIFTY-SEVEN

If you want to be a great bitcoiner,
you must start attending your local meetup.
Stop trying to remain anonymous.
Let go of your concern of endorsing Bitcoin publicly,
and the world will achieve hyperbitcoinization sooner.

How do I know this is so?
Because in this world,
the greater the perceived risk of being wrong,
the more timid people become;
the more successful the propaganda,
the more one doubts their own intuition;
the more isolated the people feel,
the more divisive rhetoric becomes;
the less understanding we all possess,
the longer the world remains ignorant of
a better alternative.

Therefore the bitcoiner says:
I teach about the problem of fiat before Bitcoin.
I don't spread prophecy but ideas.
I increase my purchasing power just from being patient.
If I keep from selling my bitcoin to stronger hands,
I can increase my standard of living over time.

FIFTY-EIGHT

When the people have sound money,
their lives are enjoyable and free.
When the government meddles with
the medium of exchange,
they become overworked and underpaid.

Ignorance of better alternatives
is what fiat money depends on;
The term "crypto" is what scam projects hide under.
Who knows when the next Gary Gensler will be hired?
Is there no definition of "blatant scam" at the SEC?
Yet a brilliant innovation is too soon conflated with
"get-rich-quick scheme" or cult;
long-term adoption could indeed take a while.

Thus the bitcoiner is content to serve as an example
and to not impose peer pressure.
His intellect is sharp but does not belittle;
his examples are compelling but not confusing;
his proof of work influences but does not force.

FIFTY-NINE

In changing the rules of the protocol,
nothing surpasses slow and marginal improvements.

Restraint begins with giving up
one's own ideas about how Bitcoin should be.
This depends on experience learned
from the Blocksize Wars.
If there is a working store of value,
then perhaps nothing should be changed.
Yet if nothing is changed, then there is no scaling.
If a man knows this conundrum,
he is fit to submit a pull request.

This is the way to become deeply aware
and firmly focused on security,
the secret to a long and lasting monetary network.

SIXTY

Governance of a decentralized blockchain
is like a finely tuned watch.
You weaken it with too many changes.

Approach draft BIPs with caution
and unintended use cases will not prevail.
Not that upgrades aren't allowed,
but first ensure its usage will not harm other users.
Only if the soft forks benefit all,
should the bitcoiner himself promote a change.

If only the plebs would keep from rushing in new BIPs
that could harm the protocol security,
all the benefits of a sound monetary network
would be shared
to the world.

SIXTY-ONE

A great monetary asset is the base layer
toward which all medium of exchange will flow.
It is the store of value of humans and machines alike,
the denominator of all transactions.
Bitcoin overcomes fiat dominance through survival,
by remaining a constant through the storm.

So if a fiat government follows bitcoiners,
they'll start stacking bits and see progress.
If bitcoiners orange-pill a great nation,
they will enrich that nation and its people.
One wins by stacking sats;
the rest, by staying humble.

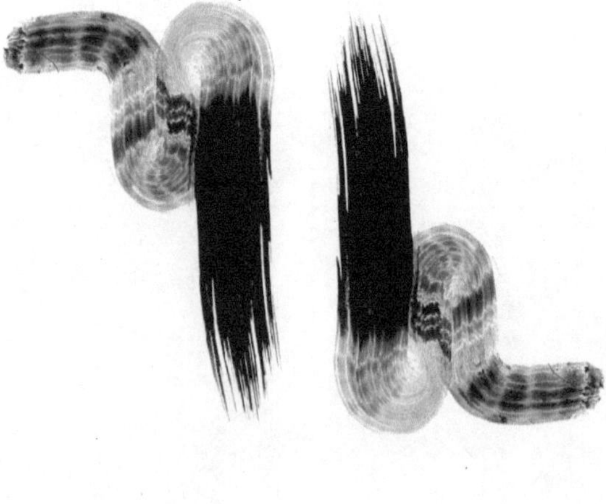

SIXTY-TWO

Bitcoin is a treasure,
the perfect monetary asset,
the secret to 21st-century prosperity.
It is the savings tool for the good
and an affinity scam for the bad.

If a person seems like they're shitcoining,
do not cast him away.
Give him the orange pill,
teach him about Bitcoin Script,
repay his degeneracy with generosity.
Do not cast him away;
cast away his confusion.

Thus when a new narrative arises,
do not try to dismiss it
with your reputation or expertise.
Meditate on the principles of sound money;
offer instead to teach others
about the blockchain trilemma and path dependency.

Why did Bitcoin OGs take so much care in
preventing hard forks?
Is it not because Bitcoin is the source of monetary truth,
an immutable ledger for all?
It is the most important invention of our lifetime.

SIXTY-THREE

Practice HODLing,
build wealth through patience.
DCA every day.
Withdraw to self-custody, back up your seed phrase.
See drawdowns as opportunities.
See clarity in the chaos.
Achieve wisdom through survival.

Build projects during bear markets;
manage UTXOs when fees are low.
The bitcoiner does not attempt to trade with leverage,
and thus understands continuous compounding growth.

If you sell for fiat too quickly,
your wealth will not last long;
because the bitcoiner always spends and replaces,
his net worth never stops growing.

SIXTY-FOUR

A draft BIP is easily submitted.
What is not assigned a BIP number is easy to overlook.
The soft forks are easily contentious;
the hard forks are easily a nonstarter.

Promote your idea before Speedy Trial;
get developer mailing list approval before going public.
Remember:
There is nothing more powerful than
an idea whose time has come.
A multi-trillion-dollar monetary protocol
starts with one line of code.
A lifetime of incremental improvements
starts with a single pull request.

Meddle and destroy it; control it and lose its value.
The developer does not create consensus forks,
and so makes Bitcoin stronger.
He does not try to "Change The Code."
Newcomers usually lose the plot
right when they're on the verge of understanding.
So take as much care as a veteran developer,
as you did in the beginning.

The Core dev does not merge unlinted code;
He does not submit a PR without multiple reviews;
he learns to express his ideas succinctly.
He helps the rest of the community
understand what Bitcoin could be
but does not claim to know what Bitcoin is.

SIXTY-FIVE

The OG Bitcoiners had a simple focus
and wanted permissionless peer-to-peer money.
They did not use "Bitcoin bridges"
or trust their funds with DLCs,
so their coins were truly theirs.

When they think they know what code to merge,
changes are difficult to implement
When they know they do not know
code can be merged

Not using forced upgrades to govern a protocol
is a good indicator of its health.
The simplest primitives are the clearest.
Content with the right to send and receive,
you can show people the way
back to Bitcoin's original purpose.

SIXTY-SIX

Why is Bitcoin king of 10,000,000+ cryptos?
Because it stands before all, relatively unchanged.
Backward compatibility gives it power.

Therefore, those desiring a stable monetary protocol
must move carefully.
Those desiring to improve Bitcoin
must first study its history.

Thus, it is when a bitcoiner proclaims
about the trappings of fiat currency,
they do not feel the heaviness of his bags,
and when he promotes a savings strategy in public,
they do not feel "sold to."

He stays humble
so the world never knows how much he has stacked.
He remains a pleb
so the world never tires of paying him in bitcoin.

SIXTY-SEVEN

All of the world talks about Bitcoin
with such familiarity—
how naive!
Bitcoin is not something you learn in 15 minutes
or is taught by mainstream media.
It is not something you learn accidentally
or easily forget.
If Bitcoin were like this,
it would have ended like the tulip bubble long ago.

I have three treasures, which I hold tightly
and watch closely.
The first, a full node.
The second is private keys.
The third, my S9.

From a full node comes peer-to-peer transactions.
From private keys comes the permissionless nature.
From my S9 comes proof of work.
Now if one sent peer-to-peer without a node,
if one claimed sovereignty without their own keys,
if one didn't exhibit their own fair share of hashrate,
Bitcoin would fail.

Aligned incentives vanquish forks,
It is impregnable to attackers.
When the blockchain secures value for all,
does it do so with an army?
No, it does so with math.

SIXTY-EIGHT

A good upgrade is not consensus-breaking.
A good core dev is apolitical.
Good PRs do not create contention.
Good miners don't censor block templates.
The best BIP follows the will of economic incentives.

All of them embody the virtue of cooperation.
This is called the beauty of elegant design.
This is called the actualization of Bitcoin's potential.

This since the first block has been known
as peer-to-peer money.

SIXTY-NINE

There is a saying among bitcoiners
I dare not spend a sat
but would rather HODL forever;
I dare not cash out
but would rather DCA.

This is called
using bitcoin as a store of value,
using one property but not another.

There is no greater mistake
than not spending bitcoin;
for when bitcoin is not spent,
there is no room for adoption.

Thus when Thiers' and Gresham's law meet,
the need for a medium of exchange
will triumph.

When two forces are evenly strong,
the one with long-term sustainability wins.

SEVENTY

Bitcoin is very easy to understand
and very easy to use;
yet so few in this world understand it,
and so few are willing to learn.

Its beginning has an ancestor,
the goal, a simple motive.
The people have no knowledge of this
therefore they have no knowledge of the solution.

This is why the bitcoiner dresses plainly,
even though his wallet is full of UTXOs from the 1st epoch.

SEVENTY-ONE

Spending fiat is sensible.
Saving fiat is futile.

Only when we are sick of our circumstances
shall we seek change and save in bitcoin.
The bitcoiner is not discouraged by inflation
but the lack of understanding of it;
this is the secret of his unwavering conviction.

SEVENTY-TWO

When the people lack a basic understanding of Bitcoin,
mistakes in development will be made.
When people do not fear recursivity,
a greater complexity will be unveiled.

Do not limit the potential of Bitcoin.
Do not despise the timing of your first purchase.
Do not resist the natural course of development.
In this way you will never weary of being a bitcoiner.

Therefore the bitcoiner studies the code
but doesn't participate in public PR debates;
reads to learn,
but does not try to influence others.
He prefers his own conviction
over group confirmation bias.

SEVENTY-THREE

Saving in fiat leads to control.
Saving in bitcoin leads to freedom.
Both of these choices
sometimes reward
and sometimes humble you.

It is Bitcoin's way to secure without force.
It does not command, yet nodes cooperate.
It does not promise, yet scarcity remains absolute.
It does not have a schedule,
yet it confirms roughly every 10 minutes.

The chain of Bitcoin settles all transactions;
its blocks are slow,
but no record is missing from its ledger.

SEVENTY-FOUR

If you realize Bitcoin itself must change,
there is no version you will cling to forever.
If you do not fear Bitcoin's uncertain future,
there is no upgrade you cannot navigate.

Yet there is always the unknown beyond each upgrade.
He who tries to force Bitcoin's destiny
is like one who alters the course
of a mighty river.
Whoever tries to alter the flow of a mighty river
is certain to be swept away.

SEVENTY-FIVE

When inflation is too high, people's time is stolen.
When the government controls the money,
people's wealth silently disappears.

Let Bitcoin restore value to people's work;
trust their choices, leave their money alone.

SEVENTY-SIX

Bitcoin was born quiet and fragile;
at its genesis, vulnerable and niche.
All systems, including code and consensus itself,
are adaptive and humble in the beginning;
rigid and unchanging near their end.

Thus, adaptability is the companion of growth;
Inflexibility the companion of decline.
Consensus that cannot change
will eventually split apart.
A plan that can't adapt
will split from its own strength.

The sturdy and rigid will eventually fracture;
the resilient and adaptive will prevail.

SEVENTY-SEVEN

The way of open source
is like balancing a scale:
When code is scarce, it is created;
When code is abundant, it is shared.

If knowledge is lacking, it is provided;
If knowledge is in surplus, it is freely distributed.
The way of fiat is the opposite:
It creates false scarcity
to profit from its artificial surplus.
It locks away knowledge
to enrich those who already have enough.

Only the one who follows open-source principles
offers his surplus to the world.
What developer has more than enough
and shares his work freely with all?
Only one aligned with Satoshi.

The bitcoiner can keep giving
because his wealth compounds forever.
He codes without expectation,
builds without taking credit,
and never believes his commits are above another dev's.

SEVENTY-EIGHT

Nothing in the world is quieter
and stronger than silent conviction.
For overcoming fear, uncertainty, and doubt,
nothing can surpass it.
There is nothing like it.

The hodler outlasts the trader;
the stacker defeats the degen.
In all of crypto twitter, everyone understands this truth,
yet very few follow it consistently.

Therefore the bitcoiner remains calm during selloffs;
FUD does not enter his mind.
Because he does not rush global adoption,
he is adoption's greatest catalyst.

Hard money is both invisible and paradoxical.

SEVENTY-NINE

After a contentious fork, much uncertainty remains.
How should one respond?
Holding calmly onto the original chain
is usually best in the end.

Someone must risk trading new forked coins for bitcoin,
or confusion will never turn to clarity.
Thus, the wise hold without worry of loss.

One who trusts Bitcoin's path
always knows which chain of work to follow.
One who lacks conviction
chases forks hoping to gain more.
To the hodler comes abundance;
to the speculator, a worthless wallet.

EIGHTY

Imagine a humble life, quietly stacking sats.
They have fiat but rarely spend it;
they savor the fruit of their own labor,
and do not chase quick profits through schemes.

They value scarcity deeply and do not waste sats.
Since they understand bitcoin's rarity,
they find satisfaction in just saving.
Though opportunities to spend money surround them,
they prefer restraint.

They are content with simple pleasures,
pleased by lasting quality,
satisfied with proof of work,
and protective of their low time preference lifestyle.

Though they see neighbors caught up in endless spending,
and the noises of consumption
are all around,
they quietly stack, leaving others in peace,
while they grow generational wealth patiently over time.

EIGHTY-ONE

True wealth is not measured;
measured wealth is not true.
Bitcoiners do not hoard possessions;
those who hoard are not bitcoiners.
Those who value time do not worship money;
those who worship money do not understand time.

The wise bitcoiner accumulates sats
to enrich their life and others;
the more they enrich others,
the richer they become.

Fixing the money will bring prosperity to all,
doing harm to none.
The bitcoiner knows it:
using sound money to repair what is broken,
and opposing himself to the injustice of fiat currency.

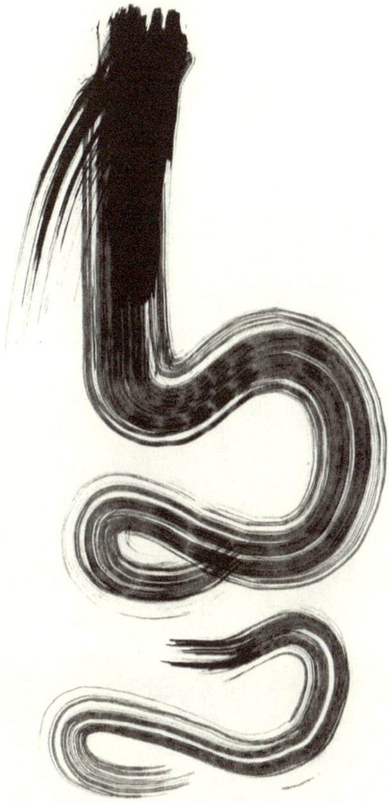

Glossary

$5 wrench attack (verse 3) – A physical attack where someone uses force or coercion to steal bitcoin, bypassing all cryptographic security.

51% attack (verses 1, 29) – An attack where a miner or group controls the majority of hashrate and can reorganize the blockchain.

airdrops (verses 12, 19, 31) – Free token distributions, typically used by altcoin projects to generate hype.

altcoiners (verses 15, 22) – People who invest in or promote altcoins.

altcoins (verses 3, 9, 12, 15, 20, 22, 30, 31, 35, 36, 42) – Any cryptocurrency other than Bitcoin.

anon (verses 20, 39) – Anonymous; someone who conceals their identity online.

ASICs (verses 12, 29) – Application-Specific Integrated Circuits; specialized hardware built exclusively for Bitcoin mining.

B-cash maxi (verse 8) – An ironic term for Bitcoin Cash supporters who prioritize using bitcoin as a medium of exchange.

B-money (verse 42) – Wei Dai's 1998 proposal for an anonymous, distributed electronic cash system; a precursor to Bitcoin.

bags (verse 66) – Slang for one's cryptocurrency holdings.

base layer (verse 61) – Bitcoin's main blockchain, as opposed to second-layer solutions like Lightning.

bear market (verses 23, 33, 63) – A prolonged period of declining prices.

bell-curver (verse 20) – Reference to the bell curve meme; someone in the middle who overcomplicates Bitcoin while missing the simple truth.

BIPs (verses 15, 60, 64, 68) – Bitcoin Improvement Proposals; formal documents proposing changes to the protocol.

BitAxe (verse 28) – A small, open-source home mining device for solo mining.

Bitcoin 2.0 (verses 12, 30) – A marketing term used by altcoin projects claiming to improve upon Bitcoin.

Bitcoin bridges (verse 65) – Cross-chain solutions for moving bitcoin to other networks; often require trust assumptions.

Bitcoin maxi (verse 22) – Bitcoin maximalist; someone who believes Bitcoin is the only cryptocurrency that matters.

bitcoin-only (verses 36, 56) – The philosophy of focusing exclusively on Bitcoin and rejecting altcoins.

Bitcoin Script (verse 62) – Bitcoin's simple programming language for defining transaction conditions.

Bitcoin Strategic Reserve (verses 31, 39) – Government holdings of bitcoin as a reserve asset.

"Bitcoiners were right again" (verse 55) – A common phrase celebrating Bitcoin's vindication over critics' predictions.

BitMex (verse 9) – A cryptocurrency derivatives exchange known for high-leverage trading and liquidations.

block rewards (verses 2, 22) – The bitcoin paid to miners for finding a valid block; consists of subsidy plus transaction fees.

block subsidy (verses 6, 28, 45) – The newly created bitcoin in each block reward, which halves every 210,000 blocks.

block templates (verse 68) – The set of transactions a miner selects to include in a block.

blockchain trilemma (verse 62) – The trade-off between decentralization, security, and scalability in blockchain design.

BlockFi (verse 50) – A cryptocurrency lending platform that collapsed in 2022 after the FTX implosion.

Blocksize Wars (verse 59) – The 2015–17 debate over increasing Bitcoin's block size, resulting in the Bitcoin Cash fork.

buy the dip (verse 44) – The strategy of purchasing bitcoin when the price drops.

Cantillionaires (verses 7, 32, 53) – Those who benefit from being close to newly created money; a critique of fiat monetary policy and the Cantillon Effect.

chain-splits (verse 2) – When the blockchain divides into two competing chains, usually from a hard fork.

chainalysis (verses 8, 27, 31) – Blockchain surveillance; also the name of a company that tracks Bitcoin transactions for governments and institutions.

"Change The Code" (verse 64) – Reference to the Greenpeace campaign that attempted to change Bitcoin's proof-of-work consensus mechanism.

change outputs (verse 27) – The UTXO sent back to yourself when a transaction doesn't spend the exact input amount.

chaintip (verse 16) – The most recent block in the blockchain.

China ban (verse 23) – China's repeated bans on Bitcoin mining and trading, which miners have survived multiple times.

circular economy (verse 25) – An economy where bitcoin is both earned and spent, not just held.

coin days destroyed (verse 8) – A metric measuring the age of UTXOs being spent; high values indicate long-dormant coins moving.

coinbase (verses 1, 6, 40) – The first transaction in each block, which creates new bitcoin and pays the miner.

Coinbase (verse 10) – A popular cryptocurrency exchange; not to be confused with the coinbase transaction in blocks.

CoinMarketCap (verses 42, 56) – A website listing cryptocurrency prices and market capitalizations.

ColdCard (verse 10) – A Bitcoin hardware wallet focused on security and air-gapped signing.

combining inputs (verse 27) – Spending multiple UTXOs in a single transaction, which can harm privacy by linking addresses.

Core dev (verses 64, 68) – A developer who contributes to Bitcoin Core, the main node software implementation.

Counterparty (verse 11) – An early protocol for creating tokens on Bitcoin, predating Ordinals and inscriptions.

CPFP (verse 55) – Child Pays For Parent; a technique to speed up an unconfirmed transaction by spending its output with a higher fee.

crypto twitter (verse 78) – The Bitcoin and cryptocurrency community on Twitter/X.

custodial wallets (verse 38) – Wallets where a third party holds your private keys on your behalf.

custodians (verses 15, 50) – Third parties who hold bitcoin on behalf of users; many have collapsed throughout Bitcoin's history.

David Chaum (verse 42) – Cryptographer who created eCash in the 1980s, a precursor to Bitcoin's digital cash vision.

DCA (verses 10, 12, 20, 27, 29, 38, 41, 43, 47, 54, 63, 69) – Dollar-cost averaging; buying a fixed amount of bitcoin on a regular schedule regardless of price.

DeFi summer (verse 20) – The summer of 2020, when decentralized finance projects on Ethereum surged in popularity.

degen (verses 62, 78) – Short for degenerate; someone who gambles recklessly on altcoins or leverage.

developer mailing list (verses 39, 64) – The bitcoin-dev email list where protocol changes are proposed and discussed.

diamond hands (verse 52) – Holding bitcoin through extreme volatility without selling; unwavering conviction.

difficulty adjustment (verses 2, 4, 5, 22) – Bitcoin's automatic adjustment of mining difficulty every 2,016 blocks to maintain roughly 10-minute block times.

discrete log problem (verse 5) – The mathematical problem underlying Bitcoin's elliptic curve cryptography; computationally hard to solve.

DLCs (verse 65) – Discreet Log Contracts; a way to create conditional Bitcoin transactions based on external data without requiring trust.

don't trust, verify (verse 52) – Bitcoin's core philosophy of independently validating information rather than trusting third parties.

double-spend (verse 14) – The problem of spending the same digital money twice; Bitcoin's primary innovation is solving this without a central authority.

drawdowns (verse 63) – Price declines from a peak; temporary losses in portfolio value.

dry or wet season (verses 20, 28) – Refers to hydroelectric power availability; wet season means cheap electricity for mining.

dusters (verse 50) – Attackers who send tiny amounts of bitcoin to wallets for tracking purposes; can also inadvertently add sats.

eCash (verse 42) – David Chaum's digital cash system from the 1980s; an important predecessor to Bitcoin.

economic node (verse 16) – A node that validates transactions for actual economic activity, giving it influence over consensus rules.

epoch (verse 70) – A halving era; the 1st epoch was 2009–12 when the block subsidy was 50 BTC.

ETF (verses 41, 50) – Exchange-Traded Fund; a way to get bitcoin exposure through traditional financial markets.

exit liquidity (verse 42) – Buyers who unknowingly purchase assets that insiders are selling; the victims of pump and dumps.

extended public key (verse 36) – An xpub; allows generating all addresses in a wallet, compromising privacy if exposed.

first principles (verse 25) – Fundamental truths used as the basis for reasoning; thinking from the ground up.

forked coins (verse 79) – New cryptocurrencies created when a blockchain splits, such as Bitcoin Cash.

FOSS (verse 27) – Free and Open Source Software; the development model Bitcoin follows.

Fourth Turning (verse 49) – A generational theory by Strauss and Howe describing recurring cycles of crisis and renewal roughly every 80 years.

FUD (verses 3, 78) – Fear, Uncertainty, and Doubt; negative narratives spread about Bitcoin.

full node (verses 12, 21, 67) – Software that validates all Bitcoin rules and transactions independently; the foundation of sovereignty.

Gary Gensler (verse 58) – Former SEC chairman known for aggressive cryptocurrency regulation.

generational wealth (verse 80) – Wealth preserved and passed down across generations.

genesis block (verses 1, 6, 21, 39) – Bitcoin's first block, mined by Satoshi Nakamoto on January 3, 2009, containing the famous Times headline.

going all in (verses 41, 56) – Converting all savings to bitcoin; maximum conviction.

gossip (verses 6, 14, 15, 39) – The protocol by which nodes share transactions and blocks with each other across the network.

Gox (verse 50) – Mt. Gox; the early Bitcoin exchange that collapsed in 2014 after losing 850,000 BTC to hackers.

Gresham's Law (verse 69) – The principle that bad money drives out good when both circulate at fixed exchange rates; people spend inferior money and hoard superior money.

griefing attacks (verse 31) – Attacks on Lightning Network channels designed to cause loss or inconvenience to channel partners.

grifters (verses 30, 31) – Scammers and fraudsters in the cryptocurrency space.

guerrilla miner (verses 7, 28) – Someone who mines bitcoin independently, often in unconventional or off-grid setups.

halvings (verses 6, 15, 21, 22, 44, 52) – The event every 210,000 blocks (~4 years) when the block subsidy is cut in half; a key feature of Bitcoin's monetary policy.

hamster wheel (verse 52) – Metaphor for the fiat system where people work harder but fall behind due to inflation.

hard forks (verses 2, 16, 29, 31, 62, 64) – Protocol changes that are not backward compatible, potentially splitting the chain into competing versions.

hard money (verses 18, 21, 52, 78) – Money with a supply that cannot be easily increased, like bitcoin or gold.

Hashcash (verse 42) – Adam Back's 1997 proof-of-work system that directly influenced Bitcoin's mining mechanism.

hashprice (verse 55) – A metric measuring mining revenue per unit of hashrate; indicates mining profitability.

hashrate (verses 3, 15, 20, 22, 23, 24, 28, 29, 51, 67) – The total computational power securing the Bitcoin network.

high time preference (verses 9, 19, 24, 52) – Prioritizing immediate gratification over future rewards; the opposite of saving.

HODL (verses 2, 9, 14, 20, 22, 24, 26, 27, 30, 38, 41, 42, 43, 44, 52, 54, 56, 63, 69, 78, 79) – Hold On for Dear Life; originated from a misspelled forum post in 2013, now means holding bitcoin long-term through volatility.

hodlers of last resort (verse 22) – The plebs who hold bitcoin through any market condition, providing a floor for the price.

hot wallets (verse 38) – Wallets connected to the internet; more convenient but less secure than cold storage.

Human Action (verse 25) – Reference to Ludwig von Mises' foundational work on Austrian economics and praxeology.

hyperbitcoinization (verses 39, 57) – The theoretical tipping point where Bitcoin becomes the dominant global currency.

IBD (verse 5) – Initial Block Download; the process of syncing a new node with the entire blockchain history.

ICOs (verse 19) – Initial Coin Offerings; a fundraising method for new cryptocurrencies, often associated with scams.

inscriptions (verses 5, 9, 11) – Data embedded in Bitcoin transactions using the Ordinals protocol.

KYC (verses 7, 14, 27) – Know Your Customer; identity verification required by regulated exchanges.

lambos (verse 52) – Lamborghinis; a symbol of crypto excess and high time preference behavior.

Laszlo (verse 8) – Laszlo Hanyecz, who made the first real-world Bitcoin purchase: 10,000 BTC for two pizzas on May 22, 2010.

leverage (verses 9, 20, 24, 29, 63) – Borrowing to amplify trading positions; extremely risky and a common way to lose bitcoin.

Lightning (verses 10, 11) – A second-layer payment network for fast, cheap Bitcoin transactions.

longest chain (verses 2, 8, 35) – The valid blockchain with the most cumulative proof of work; the source of truth in Bitcoin.

low time preference (verses 1, 6, 30, 54, 80) – Prioritizing future rewards over immediate gratification; the mindset of savers.

medium of exchange (verses 8, 37, 45, 58, 61, 69) – One of the functions of money; using bitcoin to buy goods and services.

mempool (verses 3, 4, 16, 20, 22, 26, 31, 32, 35, 40) – The set of unconfirmed transactions waiting to be included in a block.

mempool.space (verse 35) – A popular Bitcoin block explorer and fee estimator website.

Merkle trees (verse 1) – A data structure used in Bitcoin to efficiently verify that transactions are included in a block.

mining pool (verses 23, 32) – A group of miners who combine hashrate and share block rewards proportionally.

Moai (verse 39) – The giant stone statues of Easter Island; once used to represent value, now just relics.

monetary trilemma (verse 18) – The impossibility of simultaneously achieving price stability, free capital movement, and independent monetary policy.

multisig (verse 12) – Multi-signature; requiring multiple private keys to authorize a transaction for enhanced security.

no-KYC (verse 7) – Acquiring bitcoin without identity verification; preserving privacy.

nocoiner (verse 20) – Someone who owns no bitcoin.

noderunners (verses 15, 31) – People who operate Bitcoin full nodes to verify the rules independently.

normie (verse 49) – Someone unfamiliar with Bitcoin; a mainstream person.

NFTs (verses 12, 35) – Non-fungible tokens; unique digital collectibles often hyped as investments but typically used to extract bitcoin from speculators.

nym (verses 10, 13, 15, 39) – Pseudonym; a fake name used to maintain privacy while participating publicly.

OFAC-denier (verse 28) – A miner who does not censor transactions from government-sanctioned addresses.

OG (verses 15, 26, 27, 30, 42, 65) – Original gangster; an early Bitcoin adopter with deep experience and wisdom from multiple halvings.

once-in-a-species (verses 50, 56) – A phrase describing Bitcoin's unique significance in human history; a monetary invention that happens only once.

OpenSats (verse 31) – A nonprofit organization that funds Bitcoin and open source software development.

orange coin (verses 20, 35) – Slang for bitcoin, referencing its logo color.

orange pill (verses 61, 62) – Converting someone to Bitcoin; derived from The Matrix red pill metaphor.

Ordinals (verse 5) – A protocol for inscribing data onto individual satoshis, creating Bitcoin-native digital artifacts.

overclocking (verses 23, 29) – Running mining hardware faster than its rated speed to increase hashrate.

panic selling (verse 44) – Selling bitcoin out of fear during price drops; weak hands behavior.

path dependency (verse 62) – The concept that Bitcoin's history constrains its possible futures; past decisions shape current options.

Patoshi (verse 28) – The distinctive mining pattern in early blocks believed to belong to Satoshi Nakamoto.

permissionless (verses 65, 67) – Requiring no approval from any authority to use; a key property of Bitcoin.

pleb (verses 5, 20, 22, 28, 34, 39, 49, 60, 66) – An everyday bitcoiner without special status; used affectionately within the community.

pool (verses 22, 28, 55) – A mining pool; miners combine hashrate and share block rewards proportionally.

pre-mines (verse 42) – Tokens created before public launch and kept by founders; a red flag for scams.

proof of work (verses 18, 58, 67, 80) – Bitcoin's consensus mechanism where miners expend energy to secure the network and earn rewards.

PRs (verses 64, 68, 72) – Pull requests; proposed code changes submitted for peer review.

PSBT (verses 11, 38) – Partially Signed Bitcoin Transaction; a format for passing unsigned transactions between wallets and signing devices.

pull request (verses 10, 59, 64) – A proposed code change on GitHub for peer review before merging.

pump and dumps (verses 13, 29) – Market manipulation where prices are artificially inflated and then crashed as insiders sell.

rabbit hole (verse 47) – The deep journey of learning about Bitcoin; once you start, you keep going deeper.

Raspberry Pi (verse 55) – A cheap single-board computer sometimes used to run Bitcoin nodes.

RBF (verses 10, 26, 55) – Replace-By-Fee; a method to increase the fee on an unconfirmed transaction.

receipts (verse 13) – Evidence, often screenshots, proving past statements or predictions.

recursivity (verse 72) – Recursive covenants; a debated upgrade path that would allow more complex transaction conditions.

ring channel (verse 12) – A circular Lightning channel arrangement for improved liquidity.

routing hub (verse 11) – A well-connected Lightning node that routes many payments across the network.

rug-pull (verses 3, 9, 30, 53) – An exit scam where project creators abandon a project after taking investors' funds.

runes (verse 9) – A protocol for fungible tokens on Bitcoin.

S9 (verses 22, 67) – The Antminer S9; a once-dominant mining rig from 2016, now a symbol of pleb mining and resilience.

saeculum (verse 49) – A generational cycle of roughly 80 years in the Fourth Turning theory.

sat/vB (verses 2, 8) – Satoshis per virtual byte; the standard unit for measuring transaction fees.

Satoshi (verses 3, 6, 42, 77) – The pseudonymous creator of Bitcoin who disappeared in 2010 after launching the network.

satoshis (verses 3, 21) – The smallest unit of bitcoin; 100 million satoshis equal one bitcoin.

sats (verses 7, 10, 20, 21, 48, 50, 52, 56, 61, 80, 81) – Shorthand for satoshis; the smallest unit of bitcoin.

Sats the Standard (verse 52) – A movement to price things in satoshis rather than fiat currencies.

scam (verses 19, 23, 24, 34, 36, 41, 56, 58, 62) – Fraudulent cryptocurrency projects designed to steal money.

scriptSig (verse 6) – The signature field in a Bitcoin transaction; the genesis block contains Satoshi's famous Times headline.

SEC (verse 58) – The U.S. Securities and Exchange Commission; a financial regulator.

seed phrase (verses 5, 63) – A series of words that can restore a Bitcoin wallet; must be kept secure and backed up.

Segwit (verse 2) – Segregated Witness; a 2017 upgrade that separated signature data from transactions, enabling Lightning.

self-custody (verses 20, 41, 50, 52, 54, 56, 63) – Holding your own bitcoin with your own private keys; not trusting third parties.

sell your chairs (verse 56) – A meme about going all-in on bitcoin and eliminating unnecessary expenses.

selling the rip (verse 29) – Selling during price increases rather than buying more.

shitcoiners (verses 19, 24, 49) – People who invest in altcoins; used pejoratively.

shitcoinery (verses 19, 24, 62) – Behavior associated with altcoins and speculation; trading, chasing pumps, etc.

signaling period (verse 12) – The time when miners signal support for a proposed soft fork upgrade.

six confirmations (verses 9, 20, 28) – The standard number of confirmations considered secure for large transactions.

soft fork (verses 15, 60, 64) – A backward-compatible protocol upgrade that tightens the rules.

solo miner (verses 23, 28) – Someone who mines without joining a pool, receiving the full block reward when successful.

sound money (verses 5, 10, 25, 34, 37, 47, 58, 62, 81) – Money with properties that make it a reliable store of value; hard to produce, easy to verify.

Sovereign Individual (verses 38, 49) – A book by Davidson and Rees-Mogg predicting the rise of individual sovereignty through technology.

sovereign node (verse 13) – A full node run independently to verify consensus without trusting others.

Speedy Trial (verses 29, 64) – A soft fork activation method used for the Taproot upgrade in 2021.

stack (verses 20, 21, 27, 52, 56, 80) – One's bitcoin holdings; accumulated sats.

stacker (verse 78) – Someone who accumulates bitcoin regularly.

stacking sats (verses 20, 21, 48, 56, 61, 80) – Regularly accumulating small amounts of bitcoin over time.

stays humble (verses 61, 66) – Part of the phrase "stay humble, stack sats"; maintaining humility about one's holdings.

store of value (verses 21, 59, 61, 69) – One of money's functions; preserving purchasing power over time.

stronger hands (verse 57) – Those with greater conviction who buy from weaker hands during dips.

sub-sat/vB (verse 2) – Fee rates below one satoshi per virtual byte; very low fee environment.

supply cap (verse 45) – Bitcoin's limit of 21 million coins; the foundation of its scarcity.

Taproot (verse 5) – A 2021 upgrade improving Bitcoin's privacy and smart contract capabilities.

The 7th Property (verse 47) – A book by Eric Yakes exploring Bitcoin's monetary properties.

Thiers' Law (verses 42, 69) – The principle that good money drives out bad when people have a choice of currencies.

Tick tock, next block (verse 17) – A phrase celebrating Bitcoin's reliability; blocks keep coming regardless of external events.

timechain (verse 1) – Satoshi's original term for the blockchain; emphasizes the time-ordering function.

tokenomics (verse 19) – The economic design of a cryptocurrency token; often associated with altcoin schemes.

treasury companies (verse 50) – Companies like Strategy that hold bitcoin on their balance sheet as a reserve asset.

tulip bubble (verse 67) – The 17th-century Dutch speculation mania; often used dismissively by Bitcoin critics.

Turing incompleteness (verse 15) – Bitcoin Script's intentional limitation preventing complex loops; a security feature.

UTXO (verses 2, 3, 5, 8, 10, 11, 14, 20, 24, 25, 27, 35, 37, 40, 41, 63, 70) – Unspent Transaction Output; the fundamental unit of bitcoin ownership.

VC money (verse 36) – Venture capital investment; often seen as corrupting when it enters cryptocurrency projects.

weak hands (verse 3) – Those who sell during price dips; low conviction holders.

whale (verses 22, 34) – Someone who holds a large amount of bitcoin.

Wholecoiners (verse 39) – Those who own at least one full bitcoin.

whitepaper (verse 33) – Satoshi Nakamoto's 2008 paper describing Bitcoin; the founding document.

witness data (verses 5, 7) – The signature data in a Bitcoin transaction, segregated by the Segwit upgrade.

X (verses 9, 53) – The social media platform formerly known as Twitter.

yield (verses 17, 32, 50) – Interest earned on deposited bitcoin; often associated with collapsed lending platforms.

YOLO (verse 29) – You Only Live Once; going all-in recklessly or with full conviction.

zero fiat (verses 41, 48) – The goal of converting all fiat currency to bitcoin.

Zero-conf (verse 20) – Trusting a transaction with zero confirmations; risky but sometimes used for small amounts.

Recommended Reading

Philosophy and the Way

1. *Tao Te Ching.* Various translations.
2. *The Way of Zen.* Alan Watts.
3. *Meditations.* Marcus Aurelius.
4. *Zen and the Art of Motorcycle Maintenance.* Robert M. Pirsig.
5. *You Are Here.* Thich Nhat Hanh.

Bitcoin

1. *The Bitcoin Standard.* Saifedean Ammous.
2. *21 Lessons.* Gigi.
3. *Broken Money.* Lyn Alden.
4. *The 7th Property.* Eric Yakes.
5. *Bitcoin Mining Heat Reuse.* Tyler Stevens.

Money and Economics

1. *Economics in One Lesson.* Henry Hazlitt.
2. *What Has Government Done to Our Money?* Murray N. Rothbard.
3. *The Creature from Jekyll Island.* G. Edward Griffin.
4. *When Money Dies.* Adam Fergusson.
5. *The Ethics of Money Production.* Jörg Guido Hülsmann.

Society and the Future

1. *The Sovereign Individual.* James Dale Davidson and William Rees-Mogg.
2. *The Price of Tomorrow.* Jeff Booth.
3. *The Fourth Turning Is Here.* Neil Howe.
4. *The Bitcoin-Dollar.* Mark Goodwin.

About the Author

Zach Wischler is a former financial advisor turned sovereignty maximalist and community builder. He co-founded and served as inaugural Chairman of The Space—Denver's nonprofit Bitcoin hub—and organized the Denver BitDevs meetup from 2022 to 2024. He works as Director of Sales at Casa. His debut book, *The Bitcoin Tao* (2026), distills 81 verses of practical, principled wisdom for anyone seeking to live well, think clearly, and build a resilient life in a Bitcoin-denominated world.

www.ingramcontent.com/pod-product-compliance
Lightning Source LLC
LaVergne TN
LVHW090413210926
848480LV00002B/547